⬤What people are saying⬤
about Terry Gray:

"Very Empowering, best class I have ever attended!"

-Kevin Williamson (American Airlines)

"Fantastic Energy and great message to inspire all employees"

-Vinnie Ilacqua (Morton Salt Company)

"Motivational; Attention grabbing; Lot's of people need this message."

-Taryn Thomas (Valero Company)

"Love the enthusiasm! Thanks for showing you don't have to be a "Safety-Man" to promote safety! Very Engaging and personal"

-Mike Rice (Norfolk Naval Shipyard)

July 2019

Published by Final Step Publishing

P.O. Box 1447

Suffolk, VA 23439

www.finalsteppublishing.com

For Worldwide Distribution

Printed in USA.

ISBN: 978-1-7331469-4-4

THE SAFETY MAN
MOVEMENT

Terry D. Gray

Final Step
publishing

⚏Dedication⚏

I would like to dedicate this book to the lives of the workers whose families we, as a workforce, have failed to protect and save due to our failure to sooner recognize the need for safety. This is for those who had to suffer because "Safety First" was a slogan and not a value. To all the family and friends who have suffered because cost and schedule made us overlook the hazards that could have been caught if we had thought about people over product. This is for the future workers that will be our children and our children's children. Safety is your job and we are working hard to make your future workplace a safer workplace.

⪮Acknowledgements⪯

I would like to first thank the Lord Jesus Christ for the chance to live and share this message with others, to hopefully inspire and change the life of someone who will save the life of someone else. I want to thank my family for supporting me through this continued journey that sometimes requires that I am away from them. Thank you to my wife Valerie for being a great support and voice of reason in my life who keeps me grounded and focused. I would like to thank my Newport News Shipbuilding Leaders and friends for cultivating people, such as myself who go beyond the call of duty, and affording me the opportunity to share this message. I would like to thank the Voluntary Protection Program Participants Association (VPPPA) for supplying so many opportunities for me to cascade this message to workers around the country and around the world. What you do for the safety industry is priceless. Last but not least, I would like to thank my mentors and supporters who have had a direct impact in my life to do my best and not give up even when things weren't going the way we wished they would. You are the best and… You Rock!! Please enjoy the message and share it with everyone you know! Thank you.

Terry D. Gray

Table of Contents

GIVE YOURSELF A HAND

DO ME A favor! Stop reading for a second and give yourself a round of applause! I ask you to do this for several reasons. One of those reasons is that we don't celebrate ourselves and all that we bring to the table enough. Think about your favorite sports team, and think of how excited you get when that team is doing well. You might scream or jump up and down because they scored a single point! You buy the apparel and you proudly speak about them to your friends and family.

We express this gratitude for these different organizations, but the bottom line is that none of these teams or players are paying your bills! They are not putting your children through school, putting food on your table, or even showing up for the holidays. We get so excited for those who don't contribute to the challenges and successes you confront and conquer every day. We tend to put the person who does all those things on the back burner, and that person is YOU!! You are making the greatest difference in your life because what you produce is what you enjoy. You deserve a standing ovation for all the lives you are changing and the differences you are making. So again I say to you, take a moment and appreciate yourself because you deserve to be celebrated.

The Second reason I want you to give yourself a hand is because you either purchased this book or were given this book, and you have decided to read it! To me this means that you are an individual who wants to make change and make a positive difference in the lives of those around you. Selfless acts of kindness and self-improvement are key factors in changing culture for the better.

It is important to care for yourself so that you can care for others effectively. If you can't appreciate and celebrate yourself you won't make as big of a difference in the lives of others as you could, because you simply undervalue who you are and what you have done to impact your environment. Getting this book and reading it shows that you want to improve yourself and your environment. This in turn will improve and change the lives of those around you!

WHO I AM

FOR YOU WHO do not know, my name is Terry D. Gray, the author of this book and the founder and creator of the "Safety Man Movement." As I'm writing this book, I'm currently a pipefitter at Newport News Shipbuilding, the sole provider of aircraft carriers for the US Navy and the largest industrial employer in Virginia. I've been a pipefitter for more than thirteen years with several of those years holding multiple leadership roles for: safety, non-profits, churches, and industrial companies.

I am also a husband, father, minister, musician, motivational speaker, craftsman, and advocate for changing the safety culture around the world. As a leader, I have seen the need for ownership and sharing the burden when it comes to safety. As a part of the efforts I have put forth, and behind my passion to be the change I want to see, I was awarded the 2013 Vice President's safety award and the 2016 Voluntary Protection Progam Participation Association (VPPPA) National Health and Safety Achievement Award at the VPPPA annual conference. I have also been awarded the 2017 "Model of Excellence" award, which is the highest recognition given to an employee at my current work site, and I don't plan on stopping there. I recently was awarded the 2018 VPPPA Health and Safety Outreach Award.

THE SAFETY MAN MOVEMENT

I have been invited to companies and organizations around the world to share the "Safety Man Movement" message and now you have it in your hands to enjoy as well. I have spoken about the Safety Man Movement and have had the opportunity to motivate and inspire thousands around the globe. I speak at events and with groups in a powerful highly energized presentation that is intended to resonate in the hearts of all who hear it.

I'm married to my beautiful wife Valerie, and I'm the father of three beautiful children. I am a passionate advocate of safety and promoting the value of human life in the workplace and in the community. I believe we all have the power to make a difference where we are. As I stated before, I am the founder and driving force of "The Safety Man Movement," and I want to do my best to convince the masses to understand that *"The safety man is no longer one individual, but many individuals that are one!"* I'm striving to change and challenge the perceptions and obligations of everyone, in the workplace and community, concerning safety.

I believe that we all should care for the loved ones of others, as we want others to care for our loved ones. We owe it to one another. I began this safety journey as a safety team member in 2012 and I've been trying to make positive impacts for safety ever since. I feel that I have an obligation to do my part to make the world a better place. If I could sum up the purpose and mission behind these efforts, I'd tell you it's all about saving souls and saving lives. I'm a simple guy and I don't have many things to try to impress you with. All I have, and all I can offer, is myself and my desire to utilize my gifts to make a difference in the lives of others before it's all said and done.

I know this section is just the bio to tell you about who I am. However, it is the most important element to this entire book! So, if you skip over this part you will miss the heart of the message the I am trying to convey. It is important to remember the things that are important to you as an individual, as well as those things that are important to others, as you as you proceed through this book.

1

INTRODUCTION

A S I BEGIN this book I want to first recognize all of my readers who are a part of the safety team where you work. Thank you for your commitment to safety and your commitment to your organization. We need more people caring and doing for others. I appreciate the efforts you make towards safety culture change in the workplace.

One thing I've learned from speaking with so many people from different industries is that we all have a wide range of hazards from one worksite to the next. Some have hazards others will never have and some worksites have very similar hazards. Whatever the hazard is, we all agree that we must be mindful of our environment and surroundings to avoid falling victim to these hazards. Some major hazards I've seen and experienced are:

- Fire Hazards
- Slips, Trips, and Falls
- Stored Energy
- Chemical hazards
- Weather hazards
- Ergonomics
- Forklifts and Company Vehicles
- Crane lifts

Every industry does not have the same hazards but we all have them. Some may be more important or prominent than others. For example, where I work, we make over 17,000 crane lifts a month while some other locations don't even have cranes. The point is that the hazards exist for everyone even though they may not seem important in your industry. We must remain mindful that we are all in this together and trying to make it back home the same way that we came in.

These types of things lead me to the realization of why safety is important to me. I know it is an intentional battle to keep everyone safe. But there are five main reasons that safety is really important to me.

1) I Care for People.

I don't know everything, but one thing I know is that no matter who you are, you have your own Bio. Now I don't know what that bio contains, but I know its contents define who you are. It represents what you live for. It represents the things you truly care about after your workday is over. It's the reason you wake up early and the reason you stay late. Whatever your bio talks about, whether it's family, a hobby, or just something you enjoy, it is the lifeline of all that we are as people. You were not born a craftsman with a hammer in your hand screaming pass me a 2x4 when you came out of the womb. You were born around people you love and who love you.

Even if you were not born under those conditions, you were born to be more than what your job title says you are. Some people may be all about themselves, but the point is that outside of work is life. Work is not excluded from your life, but it is not the limit of who you are. Bottom line, for most people, is that if they stopped getting paid for their jobs, they would stop doing that job because it no longer supports the things they care for.

If you are confused on what those things may be, consider this: The things that you love the most are the things that you would do if you had a choice and would do for free. Whatever those things are, I want to make sure that I do my part to make sure you make it back to them!

I've learned that nothing ever happens without motivation. I hope that through this book, I will be able to accomplish that and motivate you to be safe because you deserve it.

2) People's Perceptions of Safety Need to Change.

Depending on who you are, when you hear the word "safety" certain things come to mind. Often people will think of accidents, injuries, PPE, policies, or procedures. Some people hear "safety" and automatically think of being in trouble or maybe even the latest safety briefing they heard. But the reality of the matter is that safety reaches far beyond policies, procedure, and your 8-hour workday. Safety is in the very fabric of our everyday lifestyle.

Consider that while you are reading this book, you are able to comfortably sit back and relax to read with a peace of mind that comes from your safety. When you went to sleep last night, you were not concerned about bombs going off from an airstrike. When you sat down in your seat of choice, you we not concerned about the seat collapsing. When you go on vacation to laugh and have fun, it is because you feel safe and secure in your environment. You see, "safety first" isn't just a cliché for work but a value for your life. We depend upon people to do their jobs every day at a high quality and to the best of their ability to ensure that we are safe as well as our family and friends.

3) I Value the Lives of Others.

It is very important to realize and appreciate the value of the people around you. I've learned that the people who create the environments that we are in present a very unique experience in life.

Take a moment to consider how we determine the value of something. Basically, it is based on the rarity of an item or the demand for an object relative to the supply that can be made. For example, gold is always in high demand but so is plastic. However, you cannot obtain gold as readily as plastic. Plastic is more plentiful than gold therefore plastic is not valued as highly as gold is. The same goes for something like cars, you can't attain a Rolls Royce as easily as you can a Ford, Chevy, or Toyota. For that reason the Rolls Royce will have a higher value than the others.

This brings us to you as an individual. You have been greatly undervalued because you have been seen as only a human resource and not the rare and exclusive person that you are. I don't care what others may say, you are the most valuable commodity the world has ever known. If value is based on rarity, how many of "You" are out there? There is no one exactly like you! You are of great value with what you bring to the table as an individual. Your stories, knowledge, jokes, character, and experience all put together creates a very unique value on who you are.

You don't only matter to yourself but also to others. The impact you make on others raises that value even more. Companies spend millions of dollars on things you can recreate tomorrow, but you are irreplaceable. I know you may have heard the lie that your job or organization can replace you. Well, in the words of the

TV show host Maury "That was a lie!" The company can always replace your "position" but YOU can never ever be replaced! You were uniquely and wonderfully made as an individual that will bring change to the world. So with all things considered and the value that you really possess, how much money should you really be making!?! This mindset leads me into the next reason why safety is important to me.

➤4) People Need to Be Challenged➤ to Care for Themselves

In todays' workforce, it is a common mindset for workers to get the job done as quickly as possible by any means necessary. This means people will put themselves in harm's way in order to please or impress their leaders or peers, or in order to meet schedule, or to save money or time. Unfortunately, when we decide to compromise how we do things, we fail to take into consideration what is really at stake. When we take shortcuts, we are taking all that we are and all that we are connected to and putting it on a balancing scale. We take the job at hand and put it on one side. Then we take everything else that we are and matters to us and put it on the other side. From here we take a risk to put the way we interact with our families, friends, neighbors, and how we experience our very lifestyles and compare it to the moment we are in.

We will risk all of this and more to save a few minute or a few bucks, and for what? A pat on the back? A bonus? Except to save another life, there is no bonus or pat on the back significant enough for you to put your life on the line. Not just your life, in terms of life and death, but lifestyle. You want to know one of the most annoying things that can happen to you that will alter your life for a good three hours? A SPLINTER! A splinter will make you change your outlook on life! LOL! Just kidding about the outlook on life part, but the idea is that your entire life is changed until you are able to get that one splinter out! You will literally create your own tweezers to get that annoying splinter out! As small as a splinter is, it will make a difference in how you were planning on operating for that time frame.

I say this just to point out that you don't have to experience something major to change your life. However, it is the small habits of complacency that bite us when the big accidents happen. The same attitude of "I don't need these gloves this one time" when you get the splinter in your finger is the same attitude that can translate into the loss of an entire limb. See it's not the jobs that you're performing all the time that present the hazard, it's the cultivated attitude of "just this once" that presents the real hazard.

So, I want to challenge you: Consider and care about yourself enough to at least have the realization of the true cost of what is in the balance when you decide to be complacent, or take that shortcut. Understand that not caring for yourself is also not caring for others around you. When you are affected either negatively or positively, you impact everyone around you. Everyone in your circle feels the results of the decisions you make and the way you perform, good or bad. So, remember how we discussed your value and what you are really worth. Make sure to keep that in mind when you are faced with a decision that will have your life in the balance. Know that out of all of the millions of seconds and minutes that you will be working, an accident is only looking for one second! That one second can change your life forever.

5) I Want People to Care for Me and My Family the Way I Care for Others.

The truth of the matter is that every one of us depends on the efforts of others to ensure the safety of our families, friends, and ourselves. No one person can save everyone else. You can't be everywhere, and you don't have all the skill sets for every situation to be able to save everyone. The point that I am trying to stress is that we ABSOLUTELY NEED one another!

Consider while you are reading this wonderful book, probably the most wonderful book you've ever read in your life, that someone you love could be in danger. Consider when you are at work and you have limited access to the people you love and trouble arises. Think of the moments in which the only thing you can do is hope that the people and things you love are okay. When you are far away or inaccessible and the only thing you can do is hope that someone around your loved ones cares enough to step in and make a difference. When your wife is in trouble or an accident, or if the child predator decides to target your child, all you can do in those moments is hope that someone cares enough to step in and save the day. To step in and rescue them from the imminent danger.

Even if you are able to call the police to help, you can only hope that the officer who shows up on the scene is ready to do their job to the best of their ability and will take as much care of your loved ones as you would.

Now consider the other side of that coin. Your loved ones are on the other side and they are the ones worrying about you. You are the one who needs help or the person right next to you is the person who needs help. Now, your family and friends are the ones hoping that someone will care enough about you to step in and make sure you are okay and that your team surrounding you will be willing to care and take care of you the way that they would. If the person next to you is the one in need of some help, his kids, wife, mother, dad, and friends don't even know your name but are depending on you stepping up and saving the day.

See, my friends, it's not just a part of our job descriptions to work safe. It is our obligation!! How can we come to work and think that it is someone else's obligation to take the time to care for our families and friends when we can't. And then to have the audacity to think that when we come to work and think that we don't have that same obligation to be safe and protect the families and friends of others. That is preposterous, selfish, and dangerous! You see, we are all dependent on one another. Your obligation to work safe and be responsible and accountable supersedes any job title you may have. It supersedes any 8-hour workday timeframe constrictions because safety is first everywhere, in everything, and on every day.

We owe our allegiance to safety to one another! We must understand that our lives are not our own. We have a false sense of control that we never had. If you had the ability to control everything, would anything wrong ever happen to you? If your life was your own, you would determine if you had a heart attack. If your life was your own, you would determine when you get an injury. If your life was your own, you'd determine when the drunk driver hits you. And if you had this power, would that ever happen?

There are outside forces impacting our lives every day, and your actions are making an impact on the lives of those around you whether you believe it or not. So, the question you need to ask yourself is: Will you take ownership? Will you do your part when people are looking and when they are not. Will you do the right thing?

You must have integrity to do your job right and not to be complacent when you have a job to do. Understand that the complacent mindset of "Just this one time" that leads to a splinter in the finger, is the same mindset that leads to a finger being cut off. Know that what I am trying to do is change the way you perceive safety and the way you respond when safety comes to mind. Being complacent is a byproduct of complacent thinking, so even though losing a finger and a splinter in the finger are different degrees of injury, they come from the same degree of thinking. If I can change your thinking, I can change your life!

2

ORGANIZATIONAL PHILOSOPHY

THE MESSAGE OF "Safety First" is propagated very well and often within most organizations. But often times we run into a dilemma in which we are telling the people one thing but they are doing another. Everyone is told to be safe and safety first, but it seems that people just aren't getting it. They are hearing about being safe, so why are so few being safe?

Well here is my thought on why this occurs. There is a popular quote by Theodore Roosevelt: "People don't care how much you know, until they know how much you care." This means that no matter how many procedures you know, or how many degrees you have, and what your title may be. People don't really care what you have to say unless they are convinced that you are saying it because you care for them and not because your job title obligates you to.

So when it comes to the Safety Man Movement (SMM) and changing the culture of safety, one of the most common enemies to a cultural change in the workplace is that the employees don't see that what is being said is actually being done! You know how it works because everyone has that one friend that as soon as they open their mouths you already know that they are likely lying! Whether it's lying about the size of a fish they caught, or hitting a hole-in-one on a par 5. They have done everything that everyone else has done but they've done it bigger and better. This individual is not a reliable source for information and not the most likely person you will believe.

The way this problem connects to the workplace is that when we begin to make empty promises that we have no intent to fulfill, our team will begin to look at us in the same way they view the lying associate. Every promise or every commitment you make is just ignored and considered to be worthless because they have heard it all before. When the team sees that your word is no good, it drives down engagement and when engagement goes down, accidents, injuries, and incidents go up. So it is important to create a positive rapport with those people and not to promise or commit to things we have no intention of tending to.

So how do we get people to change and repair the current way our teammates listen to us when it comes to getting them to truly accept what we ask of them? How can we get them to want to obey the policies and procedures that we have set in place for the well-being of the people? We have to work hard to earn their buy-in.

⬛Buy-In🛩

So, in order to illustrate how we need to get the buy-in of the people, I will describe two types of buy-in. The first type is "business buy-in," and the second is "relationship buy-in." They are different but very similar and work in the same way. First let me show you how business buy-in works.

Let's pretend it's a late Friday night and you just got home from a long day of work. You go in the house, kick off your shoes, then jump in the bed. You turn on the TV to get ready to binge watch something and all of a sudden, and not to your surprise, an infomercial comes on. The salesman is doing his best to convince you to buy the product that he is selling. In order to do this, he lets you know how much he believes in the product and then does something crazy to prove it.

We all are familiar with the process. The salesman uses words like "It's amazing," "There's nothing like it," "It's the best item ever," and other words to show you how he feels about the product. He says this super powder juice cleans your clothes like no other cleaner you have ever seen before! But, he doesn't stop there! He is so confident in the product that he doesn't just talk a good game, he shows it. He grabs a handful of spaghetti from nowhere and smears it all on a brand new white shirt! He then somehow finds some grass and grabs it and puts stains on the shirt.

After this he applies his super powder juice on the shirt, dunks the shirt in the water a few times. Then he pulls the shirt up to show you and to your amazement the shirt is ALL CLEAN again and you are AMAZED… Then you immediately order seven pails for yourself and for a close friend. You probably still have six pails in your cabinet today as a result of that one infomercial. The salesman showed you that he cared about the product and did something crazy to prove to you that he cared. You then bought in on what he was selling and purchased the product. He got your buy-in.

The same process happens when dealing with relationship buy-in when you are trying to get the one you are interested in to buy-in on what you have to offer. My wife did not just fall in love with me because I was so dapper and debonair. I mean I was, but that wasn't why. Similar to the salesman, I had to convince her to buy-in on the love I had to offer buy showing her that I care and doing crazy things to prove it. Like when we were dating we would stay on the phone for hours into the night…

just breathing... Now I don't know how you feel about that, but I definitely think that is crazy!

You may do something like take money you don't have and borrow from friends you still owe in order to buy her something special. However, I was willing to do that and other crazy actions that weren't the most logical choices, in order to get her to buy-in on the care and love I said I had for her by the actions I was willing to perform.

How does this relate, you may ask? Well, we all are employed and our jobs are a part of a business. As a part of that business, we have job titles, but more importantly, we are also people, and people thrive through the relationships we build. With this in mind, we understand that we must deal with business and relationship. The challenge is to be able to find the way to merge the two to create a business relationship. Within this business relationship, there must be a fair balance of both business and relationship. This means that we must take time to not only develop the business, but also take time to develop relationships.

To maintain this fair balance of the two, we must understand that we can't focus on business so much that relationships are neglected, and we can't have a focus on relationship so much that the business is negatively affected. The company can't treat every employee to breakfast, lunch, and dinner, pay all your bills, and give you a bonus and expect the business bottom line not to be affected. By the same token, you can't work people so hard and require so much time away from family and friends with no recognition or communication every day of the week and not expect the morale and engagement to decline.

When we think about that fair balance, we have to make sure we don't confuse business as neglect and we can't confuse relationship with business. For example, all businesses have a budget or a set amount of funds to operate their project or program. Let's say that company A has a budget of $100,000 to operate on for the year. If you want to throw a company party that would cost $90,000, do you think when they tell you "NO," that it is because they don't like you? Or is that just a business decision?

That example may be extreme but understand that just because you may not get the thing you ask for doesn't mean your company doesn't care about you. This also means that just because the company gave a company cookout last year doesn't mean the company is required by procedure to do it every year. Decisions like that are likely company incentives in order to improve relationships within teams. However, no matter what decisions are made to create fair balance, safety has to be the deciding factor, because if we can't afford to be safe we can't afford to be in business. YOU are the most valuable resource your company has!

This means that your entire organization must agree to put safety first and become vested in the pursuit of that reality. The entire organization must agree that investing in safety, financially, physically, and emotionally, is paramount because we are all invested in that same way. Our livelihoods have a vested interest in the company's success, financially. We are vested physically, because we get up out of our beds every day and come to work to perform our jobs. We are vested emotionally, because our jobs are tough and sometimes working with people is the toughest job we face. Safety is impacted by every single one of those factors. Therefore, in order to maximize our chances of going home the same way we came in, safety truly has to be FIRST!!

3

WHO IS THE
SAFETY MAN?

SINCE SAFETY IS so important, it is very important to know who the "safety man" is. So take a moment and think about it. While reading this book, I'm sure you and any other person who reads this would say to themselves, "I am." But had you been in your natural working environment, and if your job title doesn't contain the words safety, most people would think of the person whose job title contains the word "safety". And until we are at a place where everyone can confidently say "I am the safety man/woman," regardless of title, then we have some work to do. I believe we all can agree that we have work to do. When we think about the "safety man," who do we usually think about? EH&S Teams, supervisors, Safety Department. But is it only the safety department? Is it only the safety teams and supervisors? NO!

I need you the reader to say these words: "I am the Safety Man!" I dare you to say it out loud wherever you are. Smile and say it loud: "I am the Safety Man!" NOW RUN!! LOL! Just kidding.

The Safety Man Movement is to challenge us to take action, take control, take charge, and take responsibility for our actions and others. Fueled by the shared concern of the value, fragility, and love of human life. Safety is everyone's responsibility. So, if you ever want to know who the safety man is, internalize these words: I AM THE SAFETY MAN! Again, if we were to ask the average worker "Who is the safety man". They wouldn't likely respond "I am". Until we get to the point where everyone is willing to be the "Safety Man or Woman" and accept it, our work is not done. So we have a lot of work to do towards changing the culture of safety in the workplace.

What Is the Safety Man Movement (SMM)

The SMM is about changing the culture of safety. The SMM can be summed up in this statement: "The Safety Man is no longer one individual but many individuals who are one!" The drive of the SMM is to establish that it is not one person, one position, or one group but the collective efforts of everybody doing their part to the best of their ability to attain a culture of safety.

It is very reminiscent to the human body, where every single part has its own purpose, even though that purpose is different from others. Everything has a purpose and everything has a place. The fingers don't do what the eyes do. The ears don't perform the job of the knee. No, each function is important. In the same way, the pipefitter does not do what the electrician does, and the administrator does not perform the job of the engineer. However, each part is pertinent to the operations of a safe environment.

The safety man movement is built on four simple key attributes that propagate culture change. These attributes are: EMPATHIZE (empathizing), EMPOWER (empowerment), ENGAGE (engagement), and ENLARGE (enlargement). These four attributes represent core fundamental beliefs that should be foundational for driving a safety culture.

The first thing these attributes represent is foundational actions for culture change. The second thing they represent are foundational guidelines for driving a safety culture. Thirdly, they represent foundational characteristics of being an effective safety man on a personal level. And lastly, they represent foundational characteristics of an effective organization. In the latter part of this book, I'll come back to these foundational concepts to break them down in a little more detail. But before that, I would like to continue to talk about the four attributes and unpack them further for clarity and practical application. So, let's go and jump into what these four attributes are.

Empathize

This is the first and foremost attribute to be attentive to. This is where change starts, and it all has to start here, because empathizing is where rapport is created and understanding begins. We understand that the relationship between employee and company is just that, a relationship. With that in mind, it is very important that this relationship gets the attention that is due. Empathizing says, "Hey, I care about you." It is one party expressing to the other party a genuine concern for the wellbeing of those who are involved in the business relationship. There should be an effort to care for people out of desire and not just obligation. This caring for people means you do what is right for their wellness, whether or not they like the outcome.

Empathizing is different from sympathizing. Sympathizing says, "I understand what you are going through, and out of my sympathy I will let you continue on down the path you are heading without interruption." Empathizing, on the other hand, still has the concern and understanding of what you are going through, however in your dismay, you still have to do what is right. Whether that is following the policies and procedures or changing your decision concerning the situation. Empathizing is what people do when they care about your overall safety and wellbeing, not about your feelings alone.

You see, when we are caring for you or when you are caring for others, we are also caring for your family, friends, and things that mean the most to you and vice versa. You should have concern and care about others being able to get back to those things, not because my job is safety man, but because safety is a way *of* life and a way *to* life, and it is my responsibility.

Caring for people is developing relationships, and in any relationship you have to care. Within any successful relationship, a huge part of caring is developing effective communication. I don't care who you are, any effective relationship has to have effective communication. I'm pretty sure that everywhere in the world, there's crazy music that you just can't interpret. You can get in your car, and you can turn on the radio station, and you probably hear something like this: habadoo.

It's just a sound I made up and is unintelligible to anyone who does not know what it means. That is not effective communication. Effective communication is a two-way street. There is the party who is delivering the communication, and there is the other party receiving the communication. This is the case whether you are verbalizing information or typing information in an email. Only one action is happening at a time. When one is giving, the other is receiving, which means when the communication is verbal, one party is listening, and the other party is speaking.

This is only one part of the communication. Just because you heard me does not mean you understand me. If the communication is "effective communication," then when one party is relaying a message the receiving party should be able to repeat what was communicated back, and both parties walk away having the same understanding. This shows a respect for both parties who are communicating with one another, showing that you value the time taken to create an understanding for the parties involved. I could go on forever about communication but, my point is that "effective communication" is important. Especially when building any type of relationship or building any type of communication and trying to gain any kind of buy-in.

The next component of empathizing is spending time with people and having face-to-face time. This dialogue means: I need to come and see you, talk to you, understand who you are, and allow you to see me as we speak. Body language is a communication that is experienced only in person. Emoji's don't count, because emojis are misleading. No one really laughs out loud from a message that was actually only slightly funny. And when I do laugh, there are not any tears coming out of my eyes as the emoji would lead you to believe. Your jokes, nine times out of ten, are probably never as funny as a text message or email conveys. But when we speak in person, I can see you laugh, and I am able to experience the genuine you! The you that would not be experienced over an email or even a phone call.

Also, take into deep consideration the conversations you have. Every time you approach someone, the conversation shouldn't always be: "Is that job done yet?" I'm not saying you have to know their life story but you should know there is a life behind the stories. If you are a person in leadership, which we all are in different capacities, in a work environment, the conversation shouldn't only be: "Hey, you almost finished?" As an effective leader and communicator, if your communication is one-hundred percent business driven, you are hindering the maximization of your team. We need to understand that people are people, and there's more to your team than the title they are given.

Take the time to communicate. Ask questions: Hey man, is your mother ok? Is everything alright with you? Has the dog gone to the vet yet? Did your son recover from the coyotes? Something to connect with the humanity!!

It's funny that I always refer to coyotes, because when I first started traveling to speak on the safety man movement, one of my first trips was to New Mexico. Being a city boy, I couldn't believe that I'd been seeing so many coyotes on the streets wandering like cats. My mind was blown! I was only used to seeing coyotes in the zoo. Around there, the coyotes were sitting in rocking chairs on the porch eating sopapillas. This reference is so random that I tend to get a good chuckle from it. But, spending time with team members and having dialogue is important, as is understanding who people are, beyond the surface and beyond their title. When we begin to create that connection, when we begin to create that relationship, we then begin to care about people even more. I should already care about you, because I already know that you have family, friends, and hobbies, but when I begin to learn about those things, then it becomes a connection. And that gives us even more reasons to care about each other, even more than before.

The next point I'd like to share on empathizing is that when I am the individual who is expecting a response from another party, then I have to be willing to invest first. I must be willing to give before I receive. I must be the one to take action for the people first before I can expect them to respond positively to any request that I make. For example, if I tell my wife I love her, she wants to believe me. She wants to believe in something, and when I say I love her she wants an action or gesture to follow my claim to love her! When you are trying to get anyone to buy-in on your ideas or beliefs, and you are trying to convince them to side with you and be willing to do what you request for their betterment, you have to be willing to invest!

Many people try to convince their teams and organizations to believe that they care about their safety but are not willing to make a sacrifice to invest in their people. Unfortunately, most of the time they make a minimal investment yet expect top tier results. We have to be willing to put our people over profit, because the fact is companies can only profit from the people. We cannot put the most important piece of the business on the back burner and expect the company to operate at its highest potential of efficiency. So you have to be willing to invest to the point that it stings a little and make it an investment that requires your attention and significant enough that it will catch the attention of the employee. If you want a response, you must do something first!

Again, I have to do something above and beyond and take that action first. I had to do some investing with my wife before she even said, "You can have my number." But I had to take that action because I was the one who wanted to see change. I was the one who had to take that initiative.

The last thought I'd like to share about empathizing is setting goals to accomplish. In my expressions of love towards my wife, I was giving her something to believe in. When I said, "I will give you the world," she had expectations and hope. This same concept must be implemented in the workspace. I am communicating and investing in you to give you hope that it all gets better, letting your team know that the future is bright, and it matters to me that you also believe that. When I can show you that there is something that we're pursuing that we're trying to accomplish in addition to caring, communicating, and investing, it gives you expectations and hopes! So we want to make sure that safety is first and a prominent part of your teams' overall culture by setting those goals to set expectations for accountability and hope for cooperation moving forward. We have to make sure that people who think that it's ok to do wrong feel uncomfortable. We have to let the daisy stompers know that doing "safety" wrong is unacceptable. We have to shift the safety momentum so that those who do right don't feel like doing right is wrong? We need to change that mindset, so that everyone understands that safety is of the utmost importance and thinking any other way is intolerable.

So, here's a large-scale example of empathizing: My employer built a fully staffed family health center for the employees in case of any type of medical concerns they may have. It is not an urgent care, but it is setup with family doctors if you need a primary doctor, dentist, or if you need physicals or x-rays done. You can get medication from the onsite pharmacy, and they have call-in appointments so that you will be seen within thirty minutes of your arrival. And this is in addition to the onsite clinic that is already in place. Employees can go to this family health center and their immediate family as well.

In my book, that means somebody had to be thinking about our wellbeing in order to put that in place. We'll sometimes think or say, "They're doing that to save money for the company." If you said that, then you are right, because it is still business and relationship. Which again means that the actions we pursue cannot be one-sided. It is good business because it provides a measure to assist in your teams' well-being, and it is good relationship because you want to make provisions for the people you care about. So, from a company perspective the longer you last, the better off you are and the better off they are. If I can make you feel better, then you work better, perform better, and you do better at home and at work.

The expectation is that the more I care, the more engaged and caring you become. Obviously, it has a business side because if the people stop so will the business. But it is also a relationship side because the business is people driven, and people are the top commodity, and if the business stops doing well or you stop because you're not feeling well, both you and the business suffer. Therefore, understand that there's always that balance.

So yes, we need to make sure that even in our organizations and things we put our efforts into, even from the smallest project, that we are pursuing those projects and actions that are for employee benefit and wellbeing as well as for the business. You are not just building products, you are building relationships, creating confidence, making sure that people understand that you really care for who they are. Because remember, people don't care how much you know until they know how much you care or that you even care at all.

⬮Empower⬮

This next attribute contributes as much as the first. Empowerment is the root of doing the right thing at the right time. So what is empowerment in relation to the Safety Man Movement? Fundamentally, empowerment refers to giving authority to someone to make decisions or giving your trust to someone to accomplish a task without an overseer, and also giving someone the ability to effectively operate in their areas of responsibility by way of knowledge. The responsibility to make right decisions. When I give you something and tell you that I am entrusting you to accomplish an important job/task correctly, it makes you feel good that somebody thinks enough of you to give you something to do correctly.

When you think of empowerment, think of an electrical appliance. It has the ability to accomplish its job, however it will not be able to do so until you plug it in and supply power to the appliance. Once you have "empowered" that appliance, you can maximize the full potential of the equipment. Such is the effect of an individual who is empowered. The individual will be equipped with the tools necessary to operate at their full potential.

One thing that we want to avoid are actions that essentially create anti-empowerment. An example of what is anti-empowering is when an individual is assigned a job or task to perform and in the meantime the assignee begins to second guess the individual's ability to accomplish the task. Then, soon after, reneges on the decision to allow the individual to fulfill the task and takes back the assignment because they are not confident that the individual can accomplish the assignment in the same way the assignee was going to do it. So it is important to make a point to try and avoid cultivating activities that are anti-empowering. We must put trust in our training, and if we feel that is not enough, there may be a need to reevaluate the quality of training we are empowering our teams with. What we want to make sure that we're doing is making provisions for our teams that will empower them to be the best they can be. We must build people up with tools to maximize their potential.

An important and necessary way to empower anyone is with KNOWLEDGE. The famous saying goes, "Knowledge is power," and that is true. Providing learned information for your people to be successful is the first step to empowerment. It is paramount that we supply the training and qualifications necessary to give our teams the upper hand on knowing what to do and knowing what not to do. If we don't supply these basic essentials, we are betraying our teams and their families and are setting them up for failure. So we want to make we're doing the job in the right process, whatever that job may be.

I'm not going to spend any more time on the knowledge portion because most organizations do an acceptable job when it comes to supplying the information needed to do their job. But, is acceptable enough? We disseminate information, but is it the right information? Is the information pertinent to the responsibilities of the individual? What goes into someone's mind eventually is what comes out. We must have dialogue with our teams to vet the relevancy of the trainings they receive.

One thing most don't always implement when it comes to empowering is positive reinforcement. Positive reinforcement is special and encourages internal motivation. It can be as simple as saying, "Good Job". We as humans sometimes get frustrated in the work we are performing and need a little boost to help us push a little further. For example, if you have subordinates under your care, it helps when you take the time to say, "Hey man, that is an excellent job," or "Man, look at what you did here, keep up the good work!"

You, as a worker in whatever capacity you work, believe that you are doing a good job. When a person or leader comes and gives you that reinforcement, saying "Wonderful job," you at least will likely be empowered enough make it to the end of the day. This may not always be the case, but why not empower someone with your words. It is worth your time and worth the effort. You'd be surprised at what could happen. Their response may be, "You're right, that does look good. I'll stay for the rest of the day. But give me vacation for the rest of the week!" You might be out for the rest of the week but that one moment in time makes your teammate feel empowered. This applies to you, the person reading this book, or the person you're thinking about while reading this. When you feel better, it empowers you to do your job more efficiently or at least encourages you to finish that job on a positive note.

If you want to go a step beyond the verbal effort of positive reinforcement, one of my favorite things is recognition!

Recognition, in the Safety Man Movement, is to supply tangible incentives to encourage involvement. I love recognition! You can give me a peppermint, and I am excited, like, What!? For me!? Then, if you were to give me a peppermint and some water I'm twice as excited, because now I know my water can always be cold when I drink it, no matter what. For you who have never made the connection between mints and water, that's what peppermints do for you: they make water cold even in hot places ☺!

Anyway. The point is that giving some type of tangible recognition, which took some time to go and grab, means more! To take time out of your schedule to intentionally give me something to remember and memorialize this moment has much more of an empowering impact than just words. Positive reinforcement and recognition are things that empower everyone. Think to yourself about the last time you were given something out of appreciation and remember how you felt. When you feel better, you do better, and when you are doing your part, others are effected positively around you. How many people don't like to get stuff? If you love to get some type of recognition or some type of gift or something to show, why not also do the same for others.

Which leads to my last, but most important, point about empowering: SUPPORT! You will never, really walk in your full potential of empowerment if the people asking you to accomplish a task are not supporting you with the tools you need to do your job. It's a horrible feeling when your leaders permit you to do a job and in the next breath insist they didn't tell you to do it. That's not empowering is it? But when you know that your leader has your back, you can walk differently with confidence. Knowing that when you are challenged by others, you can confidently know that you have been empowered to do your job because you have support.

So when John Doe tries to make you stand down, you can call those who assigned you the task confidently, and you can keep on going. That type of support empowers you because you know you have that internal support from your leaders and team. Again, support goes both ways. Having support from your co-workers is just as important as having the support of your leadership. Your co-workers are the ones with you most of the time, and if they truly support you, they won't let you go astray. They will also support you when you have to choose to do wrong or right. The support has to come from the top down and from the bottom up! So support helps, and it reassures your teams that they have support and commitment.

Here's a large-scale example of something that shows empowerment. Have you ever met the president? Has the president every come to your job? Not only come to your job, but actually came and set up the teleprompters and podium to give your team a speech. Well this actually happened at my job. I'm going to be honest with you… I wasn't invited to the event, and I'm not sure what he spoke about. But no matter what he was saying, the point is that what we do at my job must be pretty important. And we must reinforce the importance of the employees' contributions on the job no matter the level in which they work.

So again, if the president comes, and he sets up the nice velvet podium, gets the teleprompters out, starts reading off of it, and tells you… "You're doing great," that has to mean something to those who are hearing it. However, if we as the leaders and team that see each other every day don't continue to reinforce that message, the thought of importance won't last long.

There has to be the repetitive mentioning of how important each job is no matter the simplicity or complexity. That means that you, the person reading this book, need to know that your job is important! NEVER forget that. I don't care if you're a scientist or a stay-at-home parent. You all have a role to play.

The president visiting is a pretty big deal. But, if you think about it, he's not setting the podium up at the Wal-Mart, but does that mean they are not important? He's probably only going to McDonald's to order a meal, right? Does that make their jobs any less important? Absolutely not! We all have a place in society and, above all, we all have a place in safety. For that, your decisions matter, your job matters.

You, as a leader, may not be the president, but the fact that you come to my job, the fact that you take the time out of your schedule to come and look at the work and the things that are being accomplished, showing interest and giving support to ensure we have the tools we need, whether those tools are tangible or expressive, is empowering! The work that you do is very important to the country and to the world. Give yourself a round of applause again, you are doing some great work.

Therefore, we want to make sure that we are reinforcing the importance of what we do. This goes back to the components or the different functions of the human body. Everything contributes. The person who's affected by an injury is not the only person affected. It affects everything and everyone around them. So know your powers and do your part and be the safety men and women your team can rely on!

➤Engage➤

Engagement is where the rubber meets the road. It is doing the work with hands-on activities. This is when the individual or team comes together and actually begins putting into motion the ideas or plans created using the tools that they have been empowered with. You see, it's one thing to know what to do with the information you have received, and it's another thing to actually do something with what you know. It's one thing to care for people, but it's totally different than caring for people and then actually stepping up to show people you care.

Earlier I told you that people don't care how much you know until they know how much you care. Well, if you want people to know how much you care, you must do it with your actions. You can say the words, but can you follow through with the action to support? You see, if you care for people and are empowered with the ability to help those people, but neither of those attributes results in an action, it is irrelevant.

I understand that sometimes some people may have the ideas and thoughts but not have the skillset to accomplish the task. I also understand that there are some people with the skillset to build or design anything but who have no vision to create. This is an opportunity for us to help one another by creating opportunities for everyone to participate in some way. You must understand that people want to give and contribute, but some have not been given the opportunity to do so. So, as team members and leaders, we have to create some sort of way to afford others the chance to make a contribution to our culture.

The quantity or cost of the contribution doesn't really matter, there just needs to be the chance to contribute. Your part contributes to the atmosphere of the workplace and pushes in the right direction of having a world class safety culture.

Regardless of what others may do, another major part is having initiative! There will be times in your career where you may be required to do things of your own inspiration. You may have to be the one to initiate changes. Every team needs someone to help motivate and build morale. This may be your part. Or there may be no one to volunteer to do things.

I've heard, in my workplace, that you should never volunteer for anything. Well I'm here to tell you from experience that you should always be willing to volunteer. This doesn't mean you have to do everything every time someone asks it of you. However, you should not be opposed to helping out, and helping out with the right heart. Meaning that you are willing to help whether you receive anything extra or not.

Some people hate to volunteer, because they are selfish with their time, and because they are not willing to volunteer they will try to convince you that you shouldn't be willing to volunteer. But I will tell you from experience, people who volunteer will experience things that other people never will because the volunteer is willing to do things others are not willing to do. Some people will never go above and beyond for free! The basis of volunteering is doing more or going above and beyond your duty to accomplish a task for nothing extra. Granted, you may get things for volunteering, but a true volunteer does not expect reciprocation from the effort other than the satisfaction of seeing someone in need achieve their goal.

So I encourage you as a leader, co-worker, or friend to promote employee involvement. Because everybody needs to be involved. It has been statistically proven that the more engaged and involved a team is, the better their safety, quality, and cost results are. Initiative is important because that's an internal motivation that you don't have to ask for, it is something the individual is doing because they know it's right. Not just because you told them it's right and that it was something they needed to do. We need to make sure we're examining ourselves and getting engaged in doing things on purpose.

Let's say the building you are in is on fire, then superman flies in out of nowhere and see's the building on fire. Seeing the situation, his heart is moved and he realizes he cares about you guys because he knows you have something to live for. And let's say he really cares about you and he empathizes for you because he remembers that you owe him $500 on a bet you lost. So he is going to save you! And he's just hovering outside the building right now.

He thinks about his powers, and he says to himself, "What can I do?" So he sits back and thinks for a minute, "Well I have the heat vision, but I'm pretty sure that that would just add to the problem, right? I could just use my lungs and blow a little super breath—" because he has two types of breath, regular super strong breath and winter fresh breath, that he can us to freeze everything around him, "—but that would probably give everyone some form of hypothermia." But he settles and thinks and says, "I can just do the super speed run, go in and grab everybody and pull them all out before the building collapses or whatever happens."

But if all Superman does is just float there and never gets engaged, then he's just a man in tights. And that's creepy! If you don't believe that's creepy, here's what I'd like you to do, tonight. When you get off work, go to your nearest drug store. I want you to walk down aisle number one, this is for the fellas specifically. Go find the tightest pair of spandex that you can find. Don't even make them your size, make them a size smaller. Ok, put them bad boys on and come to work!

But wait! There's more! Right before you come in, take some underwear and put them on top of the spandex. Go through the gate and see how far you get! Security will be on the walkie-talkie like, "I don't know what's happening right now, but there's a guy in tights and underwear. He ain't got no super powers and can't fly! What do you want me to do? This is not Comicon! Just run him over? Oh ok." Boom, boom. End of the situation.

Okay I know that is extreme, but my point is if you have the ingredients/attributes, and you empathize and feel empowered, but never get engaged, then the things that you have in your mind are pointless for others who don't experience them. When you understand or know that something is important and needed, but you never step in and get engaged, then who will that help? We want to make sure we have involvement, participation, and contribution from everybody.

Another level of engagement comes with management availability and visibility. It is important for your team to know that this work, which we all perform, is performed together. Teams want to know that the people giving instructions really care about the things that the teams are doing. There is a hope that they really care about our wellbeing. Being available, approachable, and conversational makes a positive impact on the engagement level of your team. Nothing makes you feel worse than when somebody walks past you like you are beneath them. As if to say, they are better than you or the work you are doing is not as important as theirs. But, for me to know that you care about who I am as a person, it matters that you talk to me about the job that I am doing. Making yourself available and approachable, those things really empower people and make them want to get engaged.

A large-scale example, which I've experienced in my workplace, that helped drive engagement was an opportunity to participate in the safety song contest!

The participants would have to write a song specifically about safety. At this point, I was just beginning to present the safety man movement. While we were at a safety expo, my team saw a poster in the building and they were like, "Hey man, we should do that!" And I was like, "Great! let's do it!" Then they immediately changed their minds and said, "Nah, you can do it." And just left me on my own and told me to do it by myself.

But I thought about that and thought, "Here's an opportunity." I was already talking about EMPATHIZING, EMPOWERING, ENGAGING, and ENLARGING as part of my message. I figured here is another opportunity to put those words into action. So this contest gives me and others a chance to get engaged, and I can enlarge the message all at once. So it was settled in my mind to move forward and make this song and try to win. Plus they gave $1000 to the first place winner, and a professionally made music video! That grabbed my attention.

Well I went ahead and made the song and entered the contest. I thought it was a great song. However, I didn't win first place. Which also means I didn't get a thousand dollars or a video. My bank account was a bit disgruntled with me, but for me it was a success. Because the intention was never the one-thousand-dollar prize or the video, it was about being able to reach more people. I knew that the Safety Man Movement message I was going to put together was important, and I needed to share it with as many people as possible.

I knew there were some people who wouldn't actually go listen, and would just click 'yes' because they were my friends and just supported me no matter what. But I also knew that some people actually listened to the song. In that, the song was a success, and I want to share the song with you, the person reading this book! The point I was trying to achieve still lives on to this moment. I can't sing in a book, but I can make the lyrics clear to you. It's all about the message anyway.

I am going to include the lyrics line by line so that you have a chance to read them. You'll see this phrase in the song: "Like one hundred over zero." "100/0" was a message I heard from a speaker named John Izzo. It was a great speech that you can see on YouTube. Just type "100/0" in the search bar. This concept basically means that each person should take one hundred percent responsibility and make zero excuses. Some of you may have heard that before, but wherever you see that in the lyrics, that's what it means.

The second thing, or the second warning, I should say, is the song says these words: CLAP… Don't!! You may be in a library or somewhere that it is not appropriate. So in case the words get you motivated, try your best not to clap literally. LOL! Pay attention to the words. The title of the song is, you guessed it, The Safety Man Movement!

Without further ado, here are the words of the Safety Man Movement Song. I will mention the Chorus of the song only once to reduce repetition.

⟩Safety Man Movement Song:⟨

VERSE 1:

Let me present to you the safety man movement.
It's not a dance or a fad but an improvement.
Focusing hard on the value of humanity,
Empowerment, engaging and enlarging to infinity.
We're changing minds to create a safety culture,
We challenge everyone to be safe like they are supposed to.
Cause we're exposed to the elements of danger.
The last life to save your life could be a stranger.
No need for anger, I think you are incredible,
We all deserve a future so I'm empathizing telling you,
One hundred over zero, you're the safety hero,
Excuses are irrelevant, that's why you hear me telling it.
Your safety is a benefit, and you have the empowerment,
To step in and engage to save each other from an accident.
So make a point to help the people that's around you.
We all have family and friends we should go home to.
Always making safety first, always making safety first.

CHORUS:

So empathize empower, engage, and enlarge.
It's time to take control, and it's time to take charge!
So clap if you're feeling me, we're changing the industry,
You're the safety man, and it's your responsibility,
To empathize with others (that's the safety man movement),

THE SAFETY MAN MOVEMENT

Empower one another (that's the safety man movement),
Engage in making changes (that's the safety man movement),
Enlarge improvements! The safety man movement!

VERSE 2:

To get our accidents to zero, gotta bring our safety up to par.
Bottom line, are we gonna work safe or nah?
If you're committed, then i'm praying that you get it.
That resolving safety issues makes all safer because you did it.
I'm here to try to show, you're more important than you know.
We're all the safety man, and its our job to let the people know.
Safety first overall, like safety shoes and coveralls,
Proper PPE, REC, and daily safety talks.
One hundred over zero, you're the safety hero.
Excuses aren't the answer, see it's your responsibility!

(CHORUS)

VERSE 3:

We work in extreme cold, in tanks, and in hot clothes,
Snot-nosed, and it's dangerous in a shop so,
You can't avoid it, it exists so we stop those,
Who try to compromise the procedures and job codes.
Don't get complacent in your everyday experience.
When taking shortcuts, it could lead you to an ambulance
And for that I keep it in remembrance,

I'm the safety man, i'll be guilty for your innocence.
One hundred over zero, you're the safety hero.
Excuses lead to injury, so try to work responsibly!

(Chorus)

End Verse:

One hundred over zero, you're the safety hero.
Your actions make a difference, you could save yourself
or me.
So, don't do it for the money. Don't do it for the fame.
Do it so we can return home in the way that we came.

I hope you can appreciate the effort that it took to put those words together to spread this message. It was fun and maybe you find the actual song online. However, my point is that the effort and creativity of the idea created the opportunity for thousands of employees to take some initiative and take the opportunity to get engaged. I took advantage of the opportunity to spread the message which will lead into the next attribute of the Safety Man Movement.

⬗Enlarge⬗

Whenever you believe that you have made progress in any endeavor that you pursue, it is always a great practice to enlarge what you are doing. The word enlarge can also be connected with the word expand, as it is a step where you enlarge the responsibility, the message, and the efforts. Enlarging deals with sharing lessons learned and best practices.

It's important that people around us are made aware of any resource that are available to them. What we do, with the resources we have, help to make our environments better. The environment pertains to the conditions in which we work. There are some resources that I may have that you may not have, that can assist and work for you differently, yet effectively help you. Enlarging also implies that we want to make sure that we're sharing ideas that we want to be widely accepted. We're spreading the safety man movement, therefore we are expanding partnerships to make sure that everybody understands that we need to empathize with one another, empower each other, get engaged, and enlarge our efforts to make people aware and a part of the cultural shift that we would like to see manifested where we are.

It is awesome to develop camaraderie with your immediate team and associated teams by having meetings and brainstorming together. Sometimes it's just great to put together a thinktank of people who have a common goal that everyone wants to see accomplished. Another wonderful way to enlarge your efforts and ability to grow is to attend events like the Safety Plus annual Safety Conference hosted by the Voluntary Protection Program Participants Association (VPPPA). I have personally made some amazing connections at this event, and it has literally CHANGED MY LIFE!!

Enlarging is also where we want to increase the efforts we are already making, like increasing the ways we communicate information. We shouldn't limit our communication to just one form. We can communicate with newsletters, however that shouldn't be the only form. Attract different audiences by changing how you communicate. Changing the way you relay a message can change your safety message dynamics.

Sometimes you already have the answer you've been looking for, however, many times, the people who could benefit from the use of a tool already available simply don't know it is available because of a lack of communication. So enlarging will sometimes have you communicating with teams that you would usually not communicate with. Thinking outside the box and outside of your department or circle of associates can yield good results. But if we never communicate, never create that information, or if we never publicize or communicate those things, then no one will know of the things that we have as a resource.

The last piece of enlargement is encouraging others to accept the new way of thinking that we are adopting, and challenging our new and current team members to raise their personal bars of expectation and compliance when it comes to safety. That means to encourage others to empathize and care like you care. Empower others to know about the things that they are responsible for, with safety being number one. Encourage people to get engaged in some capacity. Let them know that we all have to take ownership of our safety destinies. Because what you do affects everyone around you, encourage people to understand that you don't need to know anyone to care about everyone.

Everyone should understand that we are all important and that we all have a part to play. We all have a function and are to be held accountable to fulfill that function. So, challenge the people to do right, and make sure that you're getting engaged and being the change that you want to see. You ought to make sure that you're empowering people and that you're feeling empowered as well. Spread the good news of safety and make sure that the person you work with tomorrow knows the stance you take on safety. Let them know that today is not the day to sacrifice the things you live for. Be responsible and vigilant to make it home, and also make it a point to make it back to work the same way or better than when you left.

Spread that message so that everyone is on the same page and has the same philosophy. A large scale example of enlarging is the Safety Plus conference I mentioned before and a more immediate version of a Safety Expo at your place of work. The goal is to provide opportunities to share your ideas and safety measures with other teams and organizations. So this is typically a big event where multiple teams come together and show tools and concepts.

4

THE SAFETY MAN MOVEMENT

I FIRST PRESENTED THE "Safety Man Movement" to different people within our company at an expo, and now I'm sharing this message in book form. It was important to me that I try to spread this message, and now others agree. I want you to know that when I first presented the safety man movement idea, no one believed it was going to be a beneficial effort. No one believed that the concept would be well received.

Now, to remind you, I am, was, and am currently a pipe fitter. However, when you are willing to go above and beyond to make change you can accomplish what others have said would never work. I work in the field and understand things from a craftsman perspective and also from an executive view. I am an hourly worker, but that doesn't mean that we don't have good ideas. Would you agree?

They really didn't understand what I was trying to accomplish because there wasn't always an organized presentation of the Safety Man Movement. At that time, it was just promoting a different way of thinking. We were trying to implement ideas, initiatives, or improvements. So they gave me some support, but they didn't really understand what I saw and that the vision was something greater than what they envisioned.

So what I had to do was push harder so they could tangibly see more. I had to believe beyond their belief. And you can do the same thing. Live beyond what people believe in you. When you have an idea that you are passionate about and you believe is worth the effort, pursue it according to your conviction because if you stop, people will stop believing in you and you'll never get to the next level of potential. You'll never get to the next step. Never get to the next phase.

And so, I began to push my team, and we came together to purchase some shirts to brand the message and movement. We got some iron-on stickers, and I made a design and pushed it so that people could see this symbol and think about safety whenever they saw it. When we were doing this expo, I had a message and a challenge for people because I wanted people to understand that they are the hero of the day. That everyone can save lives. You are the safety man. You can make a difference.

So we presented the movement and it got a lot of chatter, and after two years of pushing the Safety Man Movement, I was able to bring the message to the VPPPA National Conference and the rest is history! Sort of… We still have work to do and goals to achieve.

When you get opportunity to make a difference with your passion, be opportunistic and utilize your resources. When I believed I could make change as an individual and was consistent and persistent, I got to a point where I was able to convince people at my workplace and beyond that the Safety Man Movement was here to stay, and they finally got on board and purchased some real shirts for us to represent.

So what I want to continue to do is challenge all of you reading this book in the same way that I challenge others. In the next few days, you may have a lot of different ideas. My story may provoke some different things in your mind. Thoughts about new things or ideas you forgot about or gave up on and put on the back burner of your mind. Bring it up again! Right now could be the moment that they're open to hearing the new solutions that you have. They may even be ready to hear about those ideas that you wanted to present before. Don't be afraid, don't be discouraged, when they say no. It may take a hundred "no's" to get that one "yes." But if you make it through the waiting, if you push through the down times, you can make a difference.

I am one person from Virginia who in 2014 had an idea that started in one city and now is being shared around the world! I'm so excited about the future and the impact I plan on making. So it doesn't always take a lot and it doesn't take a rocket scientist to make change. It does take desire and teamwork, because I didn't do it on my own. I didn't just make everything happen on my own. It's surrounding yourself with the right people and working together, knowing that there is something greater, and then working towards that greater purpose.

I told you earlier that I'd come back to what those attributes really represent. I said, "foundational actions for culture change." It's what to do. What do we want to do? We want to empathize, empower, engage, and enlarge. It also represents guidelines for driving a safety culture. Where do we want to go? We want to go to a place where we are empathizing and caring for every single person, all those employees we're hiring every single week. It means that we are empowering those people so that they don't make the same mistakes that we made. They are getting engaged so that I know that they're looking out for me as well as I am looking out for them. And we are spreading the message, so I know when they leave from under my care and they go to somebody else's care they have the right training.

I also said, "They are characteristics of an effective safety man." What to be? Each and every one of us should be a person who cares about and empathizes with one another. Each and every one of us should be empowered with information and empowered by others. Each and every one of us needs to be engaged, because the more engaged any organization is the more successful it is. This has been statistically proven. And rather than send you to a website to read, how about you get engaged and engage your peers and see for yourself.

I also said the attribute are characteristics of an effective organization. What we want to be as a company, as a family. You do understand that often you spend just as much time, or more, with co-workers than with your family. Some of you are always away. Some of you just come to work and are just going to stay as though you live there. Right? And honestly, you can't choose your family, you don't get to pick and choose who your family is. You may not like them or some of the things that they do, but you have to care about them, or at least you should. You need to care about your family whether by blood or by association. But as a company we should Empathize, Empower, Engage, and Enlarge the movement in the same way you would want you team to do. As Leaders, we have to be the forerunners and examples to those who follow us. If it doesn't start at the top, it will have a hard time surviving anywhere else.

So, to recap about empathizing. It is genuinely caring for the well-being of people, out of desire and not obligation. Connecting to the humanity of the people. Again, empowerment, to give the confidence and authority to take action on safety items, without reservation or indecision, to address and resolve safety issues. Engagement: Being actively involved! That's the key and really that simple. Enlarging: Influencing others to adopt these concepts, promoting participation, and doing more of the things we already do while challenging others to raise their personal bar of ownership and responsibility with Safety.

Here's some pointers to implementation of the Safety Man Movement philosophy. Firstly, understand that the effectiveness of your communication and commitment from one level to the next will determine the success or failure. What that really means is that everyone is watching you and everyone is looking at one another. So make a point to integrate each attribute into the current and future initiatives.

For example, we must make sure that we are empathizing and caring about people when we do things. How will this affect the well-being of our team? I love this statement from Richard Branson, CEO of the Virgin brand, and I think if more people thought like this, they would see more success. He said: "Train people well enough so they can leave. Treat them well enough so they don't want to." That is the heart of a great leader who makes success about his team. Same thought goes for the other attributes. This is what we are going to do to empower our people. This is what we are going to do to get people engaged. This is what we are going to do to spread a mindset worth sharing with everybody.

I truly believe it is vital to start with practically empathizing for people. Because people don't care how much you know till they know how much you care. So you can scratch everything else beyond the idea that people don't think you care about them. Everything else will go right out the door. Commit some time to new initiatives. Be ready for new ideas, because you and your teams may have some things in mind that you or they may have suppressed for some time, but that are ready and fresh to come out now. And now is a better time than ever for you and your teams to just begin to form those ideas into the event or the initiatives that they can truly be. You must set goals to give vision and a road map to indicate this is where we are going to start and this is where we are going. Because there're things that are taking place or are being processed for your team, but sometimes it just takes time to get it done. And so there are goals and there are things being assessed so we accomplish things over time, but attack the low hanging fruit. Document progress and improvements. You want to see that things are actually being done. Unless you know that progress is being made, documentation is really important and helps measure each phase and gauge how we are doing with each one of these goals.

Put the 'E's into Practice. Set the example. You are the deciding factor in how people respond to your efforts. Actions speak louder than words, which means that if you tell your team that things will be done and your team doesn't see you act on them, their response will reflect that failure. That means that the results of your commitment show in how the team is going to respond.

If the person above you doesn't believe and support, it is less likely to translate that safety is first or that you even believe it. If the team perceives any type of wavering or any type of fall back, they will also tend to fall back. We want to make sure that we are making and setting an example. Your people are a direct reflection of the beliefs of their leadership.

It is also a good practice to communicate the intentions of change. Let people know that we are trying to make a difference, we are trying to pursue new things, we are trying to make things happen for them and their wellbeing and the betterment of the company. Which ties back into making goals and implementing action plans to achieve each goal. And document everything, because documentation beats conversation every time. If you don't believe me, try to go to court without documentation. See if you win. And the most vital component is to continue to provide management support throughout the entire organization. Because management support is the backbone, and the support system is very important.

Some of the results we have seen from our Increased Safety Awareness:

Increased Workplace Improvements, Reduced Personnel Injuries, 43% reduction from 2014 to 2015, 60% reduction from 2010 to 2016.

That's in my location. I am not saying this to impress you, but I want to impress upon you that change can happen, that within our organizations change can happen. We can make things happen.

5

WRAP UP

S O WRAPPING THIS thing up, we all know that the potential for accidents and incidents always exist. There are more hazards than any safety department or you or I can handle alone. Accidents, incidents, near misses, injuries, and fatalities are all real and possible. So the question must be asked: Who will stand in the gap for you? Who will stand in the gap for our loved ones? Who is going to take responsibility? Who is going to step in and step up? Who is going to take care of you and your safety when you are unaware? When you don't see the danger? When we don't see things coming?

We all need to be looking out for each other today. From this moment, make sure that you are able to get back to that slide-show that you really care about. Make sure that you are taking responsibility for yourself and do your part to make sure that what you're doing doesn't affect the next person negatively. It's a body, but there's still those functions and those things that you're responsible for. So, who will be your hero? Who will you be a hero to? Who's going to end up being your hero today?

What I know is that you don't need to know who all the people are around you wherever you are right now to care about them. If you saw a little girl run off into the street into oncoming traffic, you wouldn't ask her name first, you would hopefully just step in and try to save the day because you understand that you don't have to have a cape to be a hero.

Just know that each and every one of us is important. It has nothing to do with the color of our skin but the fact that we all bleed red. And that's the only color that matters. Therefore, we have to make sure that we are caring for each and every person we encounter. Because we all matter, we are all heroes to someone, and we all will need a hero at some point. So be willing to be the hero that you may some day need! Thank you guys for this opportunity to share the message of the "Safety Man Movement" with you.

Before you go or before you move to the next part just say this one thing for me out loud! I don't even care if you are in a Library! I want you to say it as boldly and as loud as you can. Say, I AM THE SAFETY MAN! If you are bold enough to do it, and if you've made it this far in the book, email me a video of you making your proclamation to SafetyMan@TerryGraySpeaks.com.

Thank you!

Feel free to email me any questions you may have. Or if you would like to book me to motivate your team or organization email booking@TerryGraySpeaks.com. I don't generally get questions, but sometimes people will ask questions. Generally, those questions are something company specific that I wouldn't have any inside information on, but people just say, where does all this energy come from, why are you doing all these things? And for me It goes back to caring about people.

The whole thing that started me sharing this message and doing these things was a situation I faced at my job:

A guy calls me over and shows me a metal tag on the floor. We had metal tags that were no bigger than a credit card that we put on our pipe details to keep track of them. One of those metal tags was on the floor. The guy says, "Hey come here, why don't you take a look at this?"

I said, "Cool."

He pointed and said "Hey man, there's a tag on the floor. Someone could slip and fall…"

I responded, "Yeah, why don't you pick it up?"

His response was, "I mean I would, but that is not my job."

Now he was joking with me, but we understand that some people really have that mindset. The idea that I am not going to do something because they don't pay me to do it, but the fact is yes they do. But moreover, you should do it for yourself and for the special people in your life. They want you to be safe. You owe it to everybody, you owe it to yourself. And so that made me think that I have to do something about this way of thinking, and also that I was sick of being called a safety man. I was saying, "Stop calling me the safety man, as if I am the lone safety man, you are the safety man as well."

I wanted the acceptance of everyone being the safety man to be so widely accepted that I couldn't be singled out as "the safety man." However, they now call me the safety man more than my own name so that kind of backfired, but I accept it. As should we all.

Let me leave you with this one story I learned at a business convention that I modified to fit this safety culture message. This story is not my own, and I don't know who originally made it, but my version goes like this:

There was a young man who wanted to understand how to create a safety culture where he was working. And so he went to his boss and asked, "Hey, how do we create a safety culture?"

His boss said, "I know Old Man Jenkins has the answer, why don't you go see him?"

So the young man runs down the street to old man Jenkins' beach-front house, and the young man says to Old Man Jenkins, "Hey, I have a question. How do we attain a safety culture?"

Old Man Jenkins looks at him, gets up, goes into the yard. The young man follows him and repeats himself, "Mr. Jenkins!, how do we attain a safety culture?"

Old Man Jenkins looks at him and walks away again. Out to the water until he was waist deep. The young man follows him out, and as he was about to ask the question one more time, Mr. Jenkins quickly grabs him, holds him under water, and right before he runs out of breath, he pulls him back up.

The young man exclaims, "Are you crazy?!"

Old Man Jenkins responds, "When you want a safety culture as bad as you want air right now, that's when you'll have it."

Thank you guys! For purchasing this book and reading. I ask that you share it and the message that "The Safety Man is no longer one individual, but many individuals that are ONE!!"

END